GW00675782

Thich Diệu Thiện

From: Tuệ Lưu
Tô : Tú Vũ

09/28/2019

713 - 885 - 8369

Zen Master **Thich Dieu Thien**

The Power of
AWAKE

Wake Up to break the system of ego
and live with Awakened happiness always

UNIVERSAL DOOR MEDITATION CENTER
15202 Dora Lane • Sugar Land, TX 77498
www.universaldoor.org • (281) 565-9718

THE POWER OF AWAKE

Copyright © 2018 by Thich Dieu Thien.

2nd edition I All rights reserved I Printed in the U.S.A.

Library of Congress Control Number: 2017918934

ISBN #978-0-998-1608-2- 5

UNIVERSAL DOOR MEDITATION CENTER

15202 Dora Lane, Sugar Land, TX 77498 I www.universaldoor.org

Start the light. Be the light. See the truth.

FOREWORD

This book, though small, radiates with infinite loving-kindness. The words are simple, yet extremely powerful.

There are words, when written, that can lead the reader into the world of perplexed language, adrift, not knowing the way out. But this little book is different… the writer and each phrase, each word, even the illustrations, fuse together, melt and radiate wonderfully, penetrate into and illuminate the human mind, wake people up from illusions, and heavy holdings inside fall apart; from here, they are revived into a new person, full of vitality.

Students and myself have witnessed many people while Zen Master Thich Dieu Thien opens their minds to allow realization, and further shows and guides them forward. Some cry softly, some burst into tears, when turning to the page that seems to contain a full memory of their own painful past. With joyful tears, a homeless person, who has long wandered many walks of life, now finally has a glimpse of their true home. There are also people, with bright smiles in their eyes, faces brightened when Zen Master Thich Dieu Thien taught them in words what seemed to be written exclusively for them; perhaps, from now, their lives turn to a new chapter, open up the Awake world, spacious and boundless. The Power of Awake shines in each word, each sentence penetrating through the heart and mind. If not truly Awakened, how can she write like that?

No fancy words, no knowledge here, only boundless Compassion and immeasurable Wisdom, are embodied in simple, rustic words. Yet at the same time, full of powerful energy, deeply absorbing into the bottom of the human heart, soothing, washing away dirty mud, with the vow to cultivate the lotus seeds, so one day, there will be many lotuses filling the air with the fresh fragrance of Awakening.

For thirteen years, I have been working with Zen Master Thich Dieu Thien, facing many challenges on our mission to help people Wake Up. Each time a difficulty is overcome, the Power of Awake in her intensifies: very precise, unhindered by challenges, able to work simultaneously at many levels, actively engaging in any situation, more powerful and more devoted to help all people tirelessly, anywhere, anytime. Like this book, from first page to last page, every page, every word penetrates deeply into the human heart and mind, to help people return home to the Awake treasure already within, ending the cycle of birth and death.

Suoi Tu Meditation Center, August 2017
Zen Master Thich Thong Hoi

A FEW WORDS FROM STUDENTS...

We believe that the mind opening teachings of our Awake teacher, Zen Master Thich Dieu Thien, are amazing, priceless treasures, and to benefit from these valuable teachings, it is best to meet the Zen Master in person. We are the students who had the privilege of being present with the Zen Master while she wrote this book.

After she finished the content of the book, we were very happy and suggested she write some sort of introduction. We imagined the introduction would be an explanation of the book's content, like most books, in traditional writing. But instead of writing the introduction, the Zen Master invited us to ask her questions. We were momentarily surprised, but then we smiled because we knew this was exactly her style. Awake comes from questions, not answers. So the direct exchange will be the introduction to this book.

INTRODUCTION

Student: *Dear Thay (teacher, our Zen Master), you Woke Up many years ago, but why didn't you write this book sooner so that people would know about Awake?*

Zen Master:

My vow was to help all people Wake Up, not to write books. I saw that people have lost themselves so much in books instead of realizing the truth within themselves. So no matter how many books they read, they are still trapped in the system of suffering, spinning turbulently in the suffering cycle of birth and death, and cannot get out.

Books, even from the ancient philosophers or sages, only provide knowledge. If they don't know how to return to their True Selves, then forever, the more they chase knowledge, the further they lose themselves.

The day I Woke Up, I saw that all people have the capacity to Wake Up but don't know it and are lost in the illusion world full of greed and hatred. I just wanted to directly show them how to look within themselves, to Wake Up and live with Awakened happiness.

However, people usually never look back inside and doubt themselves. For example, "Why I have everything in life but I am not completely satisfied?

Why is it no matter how much I try or how much I have, deep inside I am not truly happy?" Instead, people always look outside to get more things and gain more knowledge, trying to become something that they think will bring them happiness. This only cultivates more greed, falling deeper in ignorance, causing greater suffering. Therefore, I didn't want to give them more information or more books, or encourage them to rely on anything from the outside. I just wanted to show them the "priceless treasure" inside themselves and how the stuck points within prevent them from recognizing and using that Treasure.

So I continued to Wake people up by opening their inner stuck points, until one day they began to realize the Awake Mind and believed Awake is real. After that, they asked me to introduce Awake to the world to help people believe that they have the capacity to Wake Up. I agreed, and now, this book will be like a compass that lets everyone know Awake is real and is already within each person, and that it is possible to Wake Up in this lifetime.

Student: *Why do you write a small book instead of a big book? And what is your main message?*

Zen Master:
Again, I have no reason to write a book. I just want to put this message out there, like a hint, to let people know they have the capacity to Wake Up, and if they sincerely develop the goal toward Awake, they can surely Wake Up. And if they want to know more, invite them to come to see me. Truly, I still want to open their minds to allow realization and guide them directly. I do not want anyone to rely on books, but without a hint, how do they know? This book is like a wake-up call helping people to wake up from illusions, something to grab attention, or an opportunity to introduce about Awake.

Awake is real, it exists. Awake is true and endless happiness.

Student: *Is it possible for someone to Wake Up from a book, dear Thay?*

Zen Master:
Even after reading this book, the reader still does not know how to step in, or how to open their minds, but people will believe that they have the capacity to Wake Up. Yet each person's ignorance, stuck point, or habit energy is different. That is why even if I write things out from A to Z, the reader cannot Wake Up without direct mind opening teachings and clear guidance, except

extremely rare cases. The words in this book will give people the opportunity to Wake Up, look back within themselves, and ask questions, and help people find the right teacher for guidance. For example, if you introduce Mt. Everest to someone, they know it exists. But how can they actually climb to the top if they do not have the right person who has already climbed Mt. Everest to guide them? But without introducing Mt. Everest, nobody would know it exists, right?

Student: *There are many mind opening teachings in this little book. So which part is your favorite?*

Zen Master:

My favorite one is "the Power of Awake." (Laughter.) The purpose of this book is to let people know the power of Awake, everybody has the capacity to Wake Up, and how "Waking Up" can change the life of each person.

Student: *Dear Thay, can you say more about how Awake changes life?*

Zen Master:

When we become one with Awake, our life is completely changed, because all the questions about human life that we have from long ago are answered. Just imagine what it would be like when Awake clearly answers these questions: Who are we? What is the purpose of our existence in this world? What is the meaning of life? Why do we have to suffer? Why do so many events always happen?... Then, we will no longer have fear, no tension, no conflict, no more doubt or confusion. Only deep and pure peace, open heart, joy, contentment, compassion, and clarity. We see things as they are. From us, radiates an energy that is bright, vibrant, full of infinite compassion, cheerful, lively, open, and freely moving. Relationships are always harmonious and full of understanding. Awake energy is spontaneous and moves dynamically with the conditions of any situation. We become a totally new person. That is the Power of Awake. When we realize Awake Mind, we will believe Awake is real. As a result, we have the motivation to begin the journey to return to Awake Mind.

Student: *In your life, since childhood, is there anything special that Thay would like the readers to know?*
Zen Master:
Yes. I was born knowing Awake exists, but I didn't know how to return to it. Everyday, I witnessed this world is all about the suffering cycle of birth and death, so I always wanted to find the way to go back to the original "home," Awake. Not until I had a chance to read about the life of the Buddha, did I know that he had Awakened, liberated from the cycle of birth and death. This was the proof that

helped me to have more belief and strength to ordain toward the goal to Awaken. After many years of searching for Awake teachers, overcoming many challenges, without regard to my life, and relentlessly searching for answers, finally, in 2001, at the end and the bottom of the search, I returned "home," Awakened.

The Power of
AWAKE

Wake Up to break the system of ego
and live with Awakened happiness always

We can return to Awake Mind by bringing our mind and body together to be fully present in the present moment. Turning on Awake light helps us see clearly what is happening inside us. When we recognize thoughts, feelings, sensations, and actions in every moment, we begin to realize Awake Mind.

When we practice consistently and constantly develop the goal to Wake Up, we can listen, understand, communicate, and transform any problem within us.

There is no need to try to solve problems outside of us. When we can clear the inner stuck points, we will naturally be more open, clear, closer and harmonious in relationships.

There are two different ways of dealing with problems. When facing with something, one way is to react immediately; another way is to be clear and calmly respond. If the reaction is instantaneous, it is because something is colliding with past wounds inside us, or because we cling to our perception and prejudice. It is not because of the outside objects or external circumstances. So, do not try to solve the problem outside but rather be open and clear inside ourselves and then we will know how to respond clearly to the outside situation.

When confronted with situations, our entanglement with seeing, hearing, understanding, and knowing, makes us sad, happy, angry, afraid, jealous, and anxious. We are the first ones to suffer, no one else.

When we realize that the holdings inside make us suffer, right there, illusion and suffering fall apart. We begin to open our heart, and listen to understand ourselves and to understand others. We are the first ones to feel the spaciousness, openness, lightness, clarity, and true happiness...

Having a set plan is not a problem; the problem is holding on tightly to the plan that we created in our mind. That's why when something happens unexpectedly and that plan changes, we will react, or require things to follow the old pictures we created in our mind. However, this is also an opportunity for us to clearly see our expectations that cause many reactions inside us. With the goal to Wake Up, we can easily recognize our entanglement with pictures, transform and break them. Right there, we are open and more flexible with all changes.

When we constantly develop our goal to Wake Up, our Spiritual Insurance will grow. This Spiritual Insurance will cover us when unexpected events occur in our lives. Like an ancient tree with deep roots, the wind cannot blow it down.

Easily getting lost in thoughts and habits is the cause of the negative consequences, creating a lot of suffering for ourselves and others. The first important step is to admit that this is our problem. The next step is to develop the goal to Wake Up to break the habits, so that we can easily bring our mind and body back together in the present moment. In that miraculous moment, we no longer get lost in our old habits; instead we start to recognize and doubt those thoughts or habits. This is the first step of our journey towards Awake.

The more doubt we have with our ego, space appears within ourselves, and we are able to recognize our thoughts and reactions more easily. From here, we have the capacity to face with constant obstacles and challenges in life. In our interactions with others, it becomes easier for us to understand each other and able to see people as they are, not as how we want them to be.

The more we turn toward Awake Mind, the more our heart opens with understanding and compassion for others. We willingly share and support their transformation in many ways, and wholeheartedly encourage them to develop the goal to Wake Up.

The phrase "Know Yourself" has two meanings. The first meaning is that we need to be honest with ourselves; from that, we know the truth about thoughts, feelings, and reactions happening inside us everyday. Are they real, or always changing? Are they arising from False Mind? The second meaning of "Know Yourself" is to know that we are not False Mind; we are Awake Mind. Awake never changes; it is always present in us, clear, pure, fresh, open, and has the capacity to see people and things as they are. Awake Mind is Us, so we need to go back to be with it and live in Awakened happiness.

Awake Mind can see clearly that everything in us and outside of us is always changing. By developing the goal to Wake Up, we become clear, flexible, and open to all situations.

With only one goal toward Awake, we no longer hold on tightly or follow our ego system. The capacity of "deep listening" develops, and therefore the suffering in us and those around us transforms.

To love children, we must listen to what they share and hear them as they are. Each child will express himself or herself differently, but no child is more special than another. The most important thing is to know that each has Awake Mind, and each has their own karma that we can help them recognize and transform. It is best not to speak or react right away, just watch and listen to them. If we can do this consistently for children, we are walking the path to Wake Up.

A family that lives a simple lifestyle and practices the path toward Awake can live happily and harmoniously; automatically many good things will come to them, but they may not realize it. For a family that lives a luxury lifestyle but is lost in material wealth and illusion, the result is many conflicts leading to discord or distance between family members. Giving material things to children is not the same as listening deeply to understand them and living in harmony with them; children growing up in the material world will always chase after their greed and never stop. With Awake practice, living in any circumstances we are clear and know how to share and what to give to our children.

Holding onto any concept about body, mind, and object, even what we like and dislike, will destroy us and those around us. Greed always increases and never ends. It pulls us into the system of illusion, causing conflict, fear, and restlessness. Waking Up from this system of illusion, our lives will be open, fresh, and filled with Awakened happiness.

Whatever kind of energy and emotion we put out in life is what will come back to us. The people, things, and situations that we relate or connect to are reflections of us. They match the energy that we are putting out. Are we ready for the next level that is toward Awake? With our sincere vow to Wake Up, the energy in us will change and draw us toward the Awake environment to help us Wake Up.

There are two directions in front of us. One is to Wake Up so the False Mind falls apart and we live with Awakened happiness always. The other is to satisfy our False Mind, stay stuck in the system of suffering and the cycle of birth and death. We cannot simultaneously be moving in both directions at the same time. Only with a sincere vow to Wake Up, each and every moment is the chance to nourish the Awake seed within us and gradually leads us toward Awakened happiness.

Awakened happiness is always present in us, and we can return to it and live with it if we sincerely vow to Wake Up. When we become one with Awake, regardless of what is happening, we can live truly happy every moment, everywhere.

When we hold on to a prejudice, we cannot deeply listen to what people are actually saying. What we hear and see is changed through tinted lenses, colored by the ideas already in our mind. Entanglement to any concepts and knowledge has hindered us from developing our goal to Wake Up, deepened the system of illusion, and has taken us further away from Awake Mind.

Mind and body are deeply connected, like two sides of a hand. When the mind is unhealthy, the body will be unhealthy. A body that is only cured may be sick again because the root of suffering is still inside us. When we realize the root of illusions that cause suffering, the body will be completely healed.

If our mind is spacious like an empty cup, we have the chance to receive many things. If our mind is like a cup full of water, there is no room for anything else. We lose our chance to know about Awake world.

Awake Mind is Us. However, in order to return to and live with Awake Mind, have we doubted our ego yet? Have we sincerely developed our goal to Wake Up? And have we constantly practiced toward Awake?

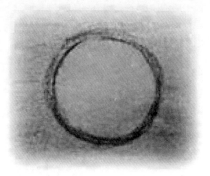

Is it truly possible that we can Wake Up in this lifetime?
Why not? Awake is your original True Self. It is your True Home.

If Awake Mind is my True Home, why can't I live with Awake Mind? It is because the illusions in you cover Awake Mind. With the sincere vow to Wake Up, you will realize the root of illusions. And finally you will realize the nature of it and break the system of suffering. Right there, Awake world will appear, and compassion instantly appears to help others to Wake Up.

Do not worry when anger arises. It's just the footprints, and it is a chance to realize the source of suffering. When an emotion arises, just recognize it, return and pay attention to our breathing, stay fully in the present moment, and develop our goal to Wake Up. Doing so, we will realize what the true nature of anger is, and understanding this helps us to soon return to and immerse in Awake Mind.

If we constantly develop the goal to Wake Up, whatever happens in life and inside our mind is the chance for us to return to Awake Mind. Not only the pleasant and comfortable feelings, but also the difficult and painful ones are good lessons helping us to realize what was blocking us from returning to Awake Mind.

You cannot remove problems that you cannot see. In order to see problems clearly, you need to turn on the light. As light appears, darkness is dispelled and everything becomes clear in front of you. You do not need to make it go away or run away from the darkness.

When the doors inside us are closed, it prevents us from living truly free and truly happy. Each door represents perceptions, concepts, or what we believe and hold tightly. In order to open one door, we need to doubt our thoughts and beliefs. Each time one door inside us opens, we are toward Awake Mind and Awakened happiness.

In life, we keep on repeating habits, following exactly the traditions and rituals that were taught from generation to generation. This is living in ignorance. Living in Awake is different; it is always fresh, open, and spontaneous. Awake Mind is always lively in each present moment, knowing clearly what to do in every situation.

Would we want to live in a house that is messy, dirty, smelly, and dark, where you are always bumping into things, not knowing what to do and what is going on? Or would we want to clean our house so that it is spacious, fresh, and bright? The same is true with our lives. We are tired, heavy, stressful, full of conflict and have no space within ourselves. Do we want to continue to live like that? If not, what should we do?

Whatever we have and whatever we chase will never be enough until we are ready to discover the truth in us. Only Awake Mind truly knows what is enough.

If we do not practice toward Awake, all the fears, conflicts, and struggles will be with us today, tomorrow, and will follow us to our next life. Knowing that, why wait? If we don't start transforming ourselves now, suffering will follow us lifetime after lifetime?

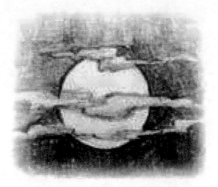

Many people misunderstand, thinking that if mind and body are connected in the present moment, it can transform all the old habit energies that cover Awake Mind. If thinking and practicing like that, do you know where your mistake is?

Realizing problems is not enough. That's why even though many times we have realized problems, we later dropped it or forgot it, and these problems continued to repeat over and over again. If we do not have a clear goal to fully Wake Up and constantly practice, how can only realizing problems help us reach our Awake destination?

When you are lost in strong thoughts and emotions: stop, return to the breath, and do not follow your feelings and thoughts in your head. Right there, turn toward the Awakened One, wholeheartedly want to Wake Up, and ask for help.

The more you look outward to gain something that you think is valuable in life, the easier you lose yourself in the chase for those values. When you gain this, you lose yourself for that.

Wherever you invest your energy and time, you will receive the results from that.

The first step of meditation is to bring body and mind together in the present moment on the basis of developing the goal to Wake Up. Meditation can be applied in any activity: walking, standing, laying, sitting, eating, cooking, gardening, cleaning, driving, working, and even while communicating. The more we apply meditation in any situation, the easier we can discover about ourselves. This is the basic step toward Awake.

In life, if you are not clear about your new direction, naturally you will easily go back to your old direction. When you are clear about your new goal, surely you will reach your destination. When you are clear about your goal to Wake Up, you can begin the journey. A journey of thousands of miles always starts with the first step, so be patient and courageous to walk. For your goal to Wake Up to be continuous, strong, and clear, most importantly you must always find an Awake teacher. Listen, so the Awake teacher can open your mind and heart, and guide. And always stay connected with the Awake Sangha.

The more you constantly develop your goal toward Awake, the stronger you turn toward the Awake world until your sincerity to Wake Up is strong enough to shatter the old habits of satisfying ego. At that time, suddenly you will have absolute trust in Awake. The power of your sincerity will carry you to Awaken soon, breaking the cycle of birth and death.

Without the goal to Wake Up, we easily attach to or resist what we see, hear, or touch. These attachments will be like seeds stored inside us. They take root there and grow strongly from our habitual, unconscious attention. This is karma. When we practice to look within ourselves, we come to understand the seeds we have stored, realizing clearly that they came into being because of our habits from ignorance and illusion. To support this transformation we must develop the goal to Wake Up.

The deeper we practice the path toward Awake, the more capacity we have to listen to our children without judgment or blame. We see them for who they really are, not how we want or expect them to be. From there we will know how to guide and support them in life with full understanding and loving kindness.

Do not wait until big problems arise to start developing your goal to Wake Up and practice meditation. The sooner you begin your Awake goal and practice, the faster you will be capable of transforming karma and habit energies. With deeper and constant practice, the Awake door will open, and all problems will be transformed.

People often think that life would be better if they were in a different situation. Truly, no situation is better than any other, and no time is more important than the present moment. We often hope changing from one situation to another one will be better. But we don't know that we still carry the problems inside us when we are in the new situation. Awake meditation will help us understand ourselves clearly, from there the roots of all problems can be dissolved. We will find true happiness and true peace in any situation.

Many people practice meditation with the intent to learn how to temporarily manage life situations to find peace. This is a good beginning, but it is very limited; conflicts and struggles continue to repeat over and over again because the root of the problem remains. But, you know, only Awake can break the system of ego completely, and right there, Awakened happiness appears. When you practice in this new direction, it will eradicate the root of illusion and suffering, and your life will change in ways you never thought possible.

$\mathcal{A}$ family or community is like a hand. Each finger has its own value and function. If one finger has pain or is wounded, we cannot just ignore it or cut it off. Instead, the other fingers must understand, love, and support the hurting one to heal. Doing so not only helps the hurting one, but also benefits the other fingers and the whole hand to be healthy as well.

You may not realize what you say and do has conditions. That is, when you give, you always expect some sort of return, and feel hurt or used if the other person does not respond as you had expected. Remember, no one takes advantage of you; only you think so and then suffer. When your capacity to practice increases, instead of reacting to the other person, you recognize what you require and set up, and you also understand the habit energies and set-ups of the other person.

When children practice toward Awake, they will not blame or pull away from parents, even though they know their parents have many shortcomings and act unconsciously. Children will sympathize, express love, and support parents. Parents are human, and also need children to understand, love, and support them. Children who practice in the Awake environment will be able to do this because they are no longer confined to the concept of "Parents and Children."

Everytime when there is a struggle between parents and children, parents tend to want their children to listen to them, or otherwise they ignore them. Both ways create more misunderstanding and hurt each other's feelings beause parents always see things through their tinted lenses (see things through their concepts or past experiences, etc.) Parents who practice toward Awake are open-minded and have space. They are able to deeply lisen to clearly understand their children, know when to stop, and when to share at the right time. Children can also apply this method. Therefore, parents are a bright mirror for children, and so this will help support children toward Awake at an early age.

Body illness is the consequence of a lot of suffering that has been stored in the mind. The more sincerely you vow to Wake Up to realize illusions, the sooner the ignorance and suffering fall apart, and right there, the body illness completely heals. Awake has the power to transform body and mind.

To start a journey, you must be clear about your destination. However, if you focus too much on the destination but are not clear about every step, you will feel tired easily on the way. If you only want to reach the destination quickly, that expectation will make you impatient, tired, and disappointed. Once your goal to Wake Up is clear, practice deeply, and right there, the Awake light begins to appear every step throughout the entire journey, not waiting until reaching the destination.

If parents have many profound changes after practicing toward Awake, their children will have huge benefits. They know how to spend quality time with their kids and when to speak or to remain silent. Their decisions are very clear and precise in response to the requests from their children. For children being raised and guided in this clear direction, their habit energies, or karma, will transform tremendously as they grow up.

Being fully aware of our breath helps us to bring body and mind together in the present moment. This is an essential first step on the path toward Awake. From there, as body and mind settle down, we can easily recognize our thoughts, emotions, and sensations as they happen. The more we are present in body and mind, the more we see clearly what happens in our body and mind. This helps us recognize clearly what is False Mind and what is Awake Mind.

The more you fear illness and death, the more you attach to the objects around you. When you lose those objects, you become more fearful and worried. It is from this stress and worry that affects your body wellness, and in the end, you cannot avoid illness and early death. If you know that your Awake Mind never becomes sick and never dies, would you be ready to step in to discover the truth? When you return to Awake Mind, you will be free from stress and fear about life and death.

Υou are not the voice in your head or the emotions or the stress… You are what can recognize the voice, the emotions, and the stress. You are Awake.

With the goal to Wake Up, we can realize and clearly see whatever happens in our body and mind. Practicing toward Awake not only transforms illusions and suffering in the present, but also has the capacity to break and transform habit energies and karma. Awake has the power to transform illusions throughout all three time periods: from the past life, through the present life, and to the future life. So the energy and the fruits of Awake last forever.

We are always looking outside ourselves for beautiful things but don't know this kind of beauty is limited to its form and always changes. We are constantly chasing after one beautiful thing to the next, never knowing what is enough. We don't know there is a lasting beauty that comes from within, radiating from Awake. It is fresh, vibrant, bright, dynamic, and spontaneous. It is a beauty that never changes or fades. It is a beauty that is so complete in the present moment that many people want to be close to it because they feel happy and connected.

Holding onto knowledge can destroy us and those around us. It is difficult for people who hold onto knowledge to listen to what others say. Because they believe so much in their ego of knowledge, they can easily cause conflict, misunderstanding, and struggle for what they know. However, if we turn toward Awake to break the ego system, and practice step by step, Awake Mind gradually appears, allowing our mind to be open, able to listen deeply, understand, and easily connect with others. When Awake, we no longer rely on knowledge; we automatically know what to do in each situation.

The environment surrounding us is very important. If everyday we live in an environment filled with perpetual negativity, hatred, and fear, we will absorb those things into our body and mind. Each day, we also take in what we see and hear, such as reading books, gossip, music, television, etc. Knowing clearly that these things will lead us to a life full of negative habits, we must change the surrounding environment by turning toward the Awake energy of our Awake teacher, and frequently coming to the Awake Center to connect with the Sangha. This helps us develop our goal to Wake Up quickly and soon transform all our old negative habits.

Food is the vital source of fuel for the body and mind. When we eat meat or fish, we are taking in whatever that animal took in, which may include pesticides, hormones, or medicines, as well as their illnesses, diseases, suffering, anger, and desires. Without Awake, we either follow our old eating habits or resist them. With Awake Mind, we know what to do, without stress and conflicts, when facing situations.

When we are not happy, we search for something outside of us to make us feel happy: shopping, drinking, drugs, eating, traveling, sex, gambling, etc. Whatever we search for never lasts and we are never truly happy, therefore we keep on searching forever. Day by day we are lost in darkness, Ignorance, and become addicted to false happiness. We may escape from one addiction, but can get caught up in another one. To truly break free from the system of Ignorance, we must Wake Up. Admit we have problems, develop the goal to Wake Up to transform all of the habits and no longer be addicted, so we can live truly happy and free in any situation.

Sometimes we lose ourselves in objects. When that happens, do not worry or judge ourselves. Just recogize what happens, return to the present moment, and remember the goal to Wake Up. Do not worry how long we were lost in our habits; the most important thing is how quickly we return home to live with our True Selves.

In Awake, ego cannot exist; in ego, Awake cannot appear.

Many people disagree, resist, and complain about others because they find their own views to be true and are everything. Awake sees each person clearly, smiles with them, and accepts who they are. From Awake, true understanding and true love appear, and we know what to ask or say to each other, without judging or contradicting. Doing so will help people begin the journey toward Awake.

If you close your eyes in a place fully filled with objects, but you still want to do a lot of work there, how do you feel? Fear, anxiety, confusion, lost, anger, sadness, nervous tension, and overwhelmed... However, the desire to work forces you to be defiant, keep moving forward, crashing into many objects, and hurting yourself and those around you. Strong myths and everything stored are still there, but unexpectedly, things are always changing, and you blame people for changing things. Then you feel limited and trapped. The lack of clarity and the limitation in your decisions has made suffering miserable for yourself and for others. These are the consequences when you pursue your ambitions, trying to fulfill the pictures in your mind to satisfy your ego. Do you want to live like this, with closed eyes, in every moment? Or do you want to open eyes to live with Awakened happiness in each moment?

To open eyes is to Wake Up. When you open eyes, you are no longer blind. You see things clearly and know exactly what to say and do, without hesitation, regret, or guilt. Even if the objects, circumstances, and plans change, you know for sure why, and move clearly and freely with those changes. You no longer hold onto what you see, hear, know, and experience from the past. You also no longer cling to the object, place, and circumstances that you think will make you happy and secure forever. Awake Mind is not entangled with the past, and does not dream of the future, so you live fully in every present moment, able to live truly happy and move freely in the ocean of life.

GLOSSARY OF TERMS

Awake Mind   *unborn, undying mind; original nature; clearly sees and knows things as they are, Buddha Mind; open eyes.*

ego   *= the "I" = False Mind, trapped in beliefs, formed by ignorance, greed, and hatred.*

False Mind   *the born mind; attaching mind; "not real" mind.*

holdings   *come from ignorance; entanglement with pictures, concepts, past experiences, knowledge, etc. in the mind that we believe are real and won't let go of.*

ignorance   *not knowing the truth, the nature, within ourselves and the outside phenomena around us; blind, closed eyes.*

illusion   *assuming mind, body, and objects of mind are real and permanent.*

karma   *habits that repeat over and over again, habit energy resulting from the system of illusions that causes suffering.*

pictures   *beliefs, ideas, concepts, knowledge and experience stored in our False Mind.*

Sangha   *community of monks, nuns, students, and lay people who live and practice together with the goal to Wake Up to break the cycle of birth and death.*

suffering   *feelings of fear, worry, anxiety, sadness, anger, jealousy, etc.*

system of suffering   *an endless cycle of illusion beginning with ignorance, developing greed, and resulting in hatred (suffering)*

Wake Up   *return to original nature, where there is no ego, break the system of illusion (the cycle of birth and death); Enlightenment and live with Awakened happiness*

To find out more about
Zen Master **Thich Dieu Thien** and
Universal Door Meditation Center,

Visit our website at www.**universaldoor.org** You can browse through information about weekly meditation classes, retreats, workshops, programs, or other special events, as well as student experiences, audio/video links, and upcoming activities.

Universal Door Meditation Center is a 501(c)3 non-proit organization. All your contributions are to connect with Awake Teacher Thich Dieu Thien and support her universal vow to help all people Wake Up, sharing this Awake message to the world. Each person connecting with Awake is a heart, a hand, contributing to build an Awake Center for many people to come, receive the mind-opening teachings, practice, and experience the power of Awake.

ABOUT THE TEACHER

Zen Master **Thich Dieu Thien** is an Awake teacher, widely known around the world as a teacher of Wisdom and Compassion. Zen Master's teachings and interactive guidance are very dynamic, spontaneous, and lively, easily attracting listeners, no matter what level of practice they have. Her Dharma talks, whether short or long, are always fresh, simple, and practical, but penetrate directly to the heart, helping people to break through, believe, and realize that they have the capacity to Wake Up. Her teachings include direct dialogues and questions pushed back towards the listeners to help the Wake Up; this stirs questions about birth and death and the path toward Awake to break free from suffering. With unconditional love, Zen Master Thich Dieu Thien has dedicated her whole life to helping people step by step Light up the Inner Light, diligently practice, and finally return to the "Treasure" already within themselves. Zen Master teaches us that when we live with our ego, there will be constant inner struggles between good and bad, right and wrong, win and lose ... which lead to fear, sadness, hatred, blame, judgment and competition with each other. As long as the ego exists, we will never be truly happy. Born in Vietnam, Zen Master Thich Dieu Thien is the founder of Universal Door Meditation Center in Houston, TX in 2003 and together with Zen Master Thich Thong Hoi founded Suoi Tu Meditation Center in Dallas, TX in 2013.

From early childhood, Zen Master Thich Dieu Thien already had deep questions and doubt about the constant changes in life and the suffering of birth and death. And at the same time, she also knew that there is an original place where there is no suffering, no birth and no death, only Awakened happiness and full liberation. However, she did not know how to return to and live in that original place. Her persistent questions about illusion life were the powerful motivation to push her to constantly search for the answer. Finally, at age 30, hitting rock bottom of her inner search for True Self, like an explosion, the system of illusions shattered, Awake appeared, and from that moment she Awakened and lives Awake. From that moment, Zen Master saw that everyone has the capacity to Wake Up, but they do not know, because they believe themselves so much and are addicted to their ego. Lost in that, they keep spinning in the darkness of ignorance, cannot see the truth, the nature of it, and therefore cannot return to Awake Mind.

Zen Master Thich Dieu Thien made "the great vow" to step into this world to help all beings discover, return, and become one with Awake Mind within themselves. Since then, regardless of their age, culture, or religion, she constantly opens their minds to allow realization, and further shows and guides them toward Awake to break the cycle of birth and death, so they can become one with Awake and live with Awakened happiness always.